Tempting Attempts of Temperance
Claudio Conenna

Introduction
Sarantis Zafeiropoulos

Prolegomena
Kyriaki Tsoukala

To my wife Marisol

Primera edición   2010

Queda prohibida la reproducción total o parcial de esta obra incluido el diseño tipográfico y de portada sea cual fuere el medio, electrónico o mecánico, sin el consentimiento por escrito del editor.

©ARCHITECTHUM PLUS S.C.
Díaz de León 122-2
Aguascalientes, Aguascalientes
México CP 20000
libros@architecthum.edu.mx

ISBN 978-607-95151-9-5

Introduction I
Sarantis Zafeiropoulos architect, prof. of Architecture

Claudio Conenna's *Tempting Attempts of Temperance* tackles the task of communing the meaning of passionate love for THE woman through words . Since, according to Yannis Ritsos (a great Greek poet, 1909-1990) *" every word is a going out for a meeting often not succeeding; and only then a word is a real word when it insists resolutely to that meeting"*, Claudio Conenna's words form an illustrative example of this definition. They have the suggestive power to engage the feelings and imagination of a nearly hopeless man in love through a highly structured patterning and movement of sound, rhythm and meaning pertaining to poetry. They keep on going out of his heart, wearing various garments, taking alternative itineraries, revealing diverse moods, uttering several sighs, always aiming at that never succeeding meeting with THE woman he yearns for. All these attempts are genuine creations made in Claudio Conenna's rich and fertile land of feeling, thinking and expressing, ready and ripe to entice anybody but not THE woman.
That is why they have to be read by any man and any woman.

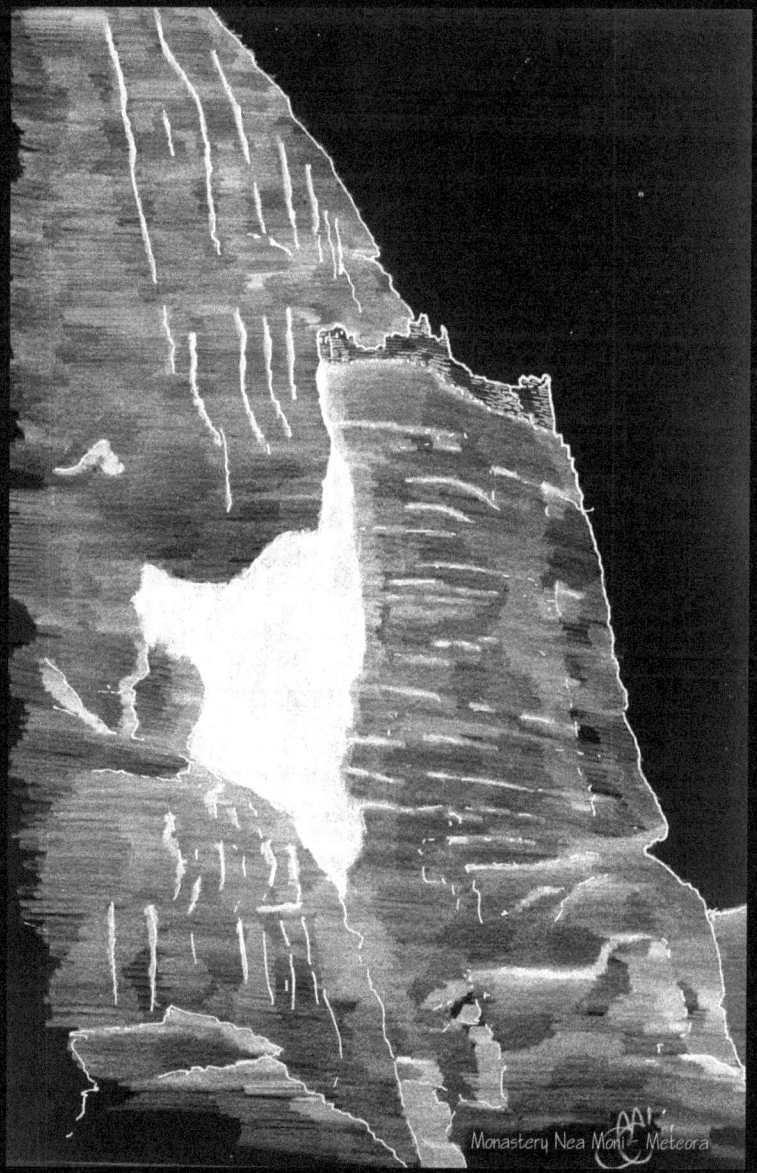
Monastery Nea Moni - Meteora

Prolegomena
Kyriaki Tsoukala architect, prof. of Architecture

Word and sketches give form to the unearthly, the remote, the inaccessible. Traces of a dream that stands out against symbolized paths of life taking the form either of a lyrical script or a visual contour. One next to the other, a strong scream of an intimate, creative and vital power. A dream and a wish that fight to hook on the real stuff, the palpable; to become a living experience; to get through the threshold of the soulful, the feasible, the actual. Traces upon paper by the remnants of symbolization, by the gist that is not a prisoner of representation, and it runs through its crevices, it gives way to the mythical, the roots, the primordial, the timeless. Traces of culminating desire, powerfully hidden within the inaccessible materialization. Trace of subversive meeting. Traces destabilizing poetics. The defined world of representation, either protective or completely restrictive creates the deficit, the void, the hopelessness, the perpetual expectation, the shout. Shapeless powers break forms and rule, they give rise to momentary meetings that fail to become consolidated moments in space time syntax of the acceptable, the established, the relieving. The impossible meeting is transformed into plural momentary tensions, reaching to the limits of eternity and routine, next to the eerie faces of desire and dream.

In Tempting Attempts of Temperance the mediation of the binding agreement maximizes the distance from the object of desire and turns it into an unreachable, cold detached and inattentive subject. Transferring the impossible meeting to the object of desire itself alchemizes the latter into an inaccessible stronghold, introverted, self-referred and eldritch. In this call of the dream and mediation becomes oblivion and the object of desire, exposed to involuntary lapse of memory, is transformed into notional essence and gets nailed down to imagination. This ser of poems culminates into the last poem where silence of voice becomes silence of death accompanied by the hope of a probable regeneration of the meeting, a transition from the impossible to the possible, from the unreal to the real.

If all the above form an interpretation of the poems, another one might be the case where the agreement is not the poet's secret, but the remaining deficit of the symbolization of the dream. In this excruciating short-handed relation of representation with imaginary reflection, the former fails to appropriate the depth of the latter. This gap is imprinted upon all poems as the impossible meeting, the alien image, the distant female form, hooked persistently to imagination, unyielding to the call for a descriptive act similar to the poet's desire .These interpretative attempts do not end the amplitude of other interpretations. Versions are many in order to recall that peculiar thing which can not be resolved by practice, the sanctuary of thought, the non-illustrative but built-in deeply within ourselves, the one that balances to the limits of real-unreal. Lady Arch is the symbol of the Rule that lives within us, perhaps of the Archi-tecture that is called to give her a Shelter.

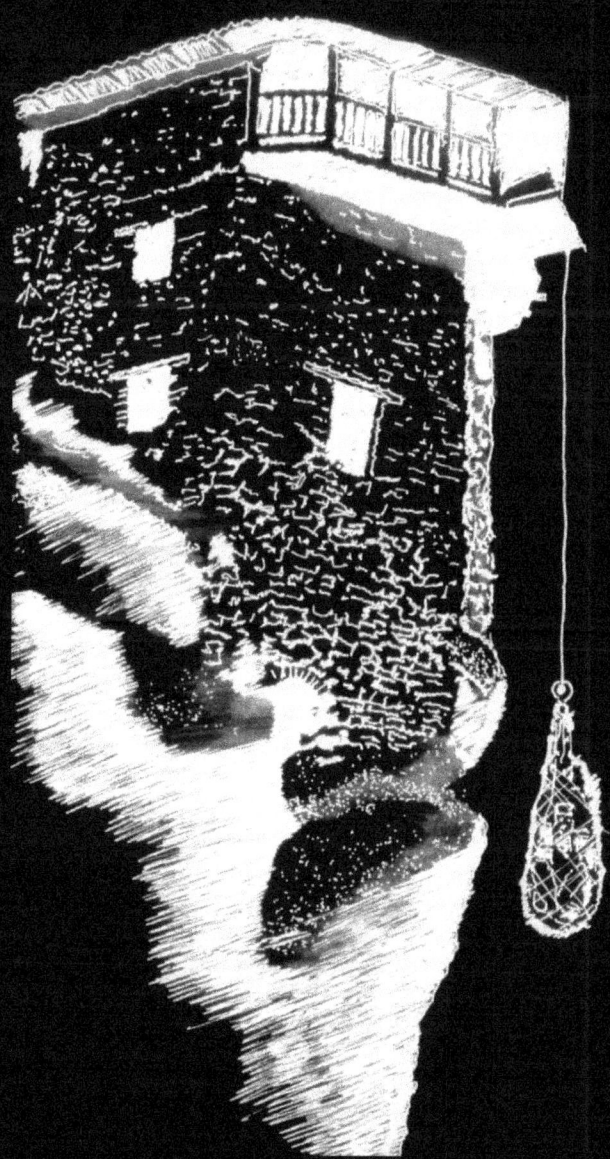

Monastery Ag. Nikolas Anapavsas - Meteora

I

...The immensity of the sea looks so green today
the color of your eyes is reflected over there
they are in the sky, shinning like the sun.

If I could cherish the hope of your presence
like the sea does, waiting for the caresses of the wind.

If I could capture the deepness of your gaze
like the earth seizes the warmth of the sun's rays.
What an illusion... I'd like to meet you.

You are like the light of a thunderbolt
so strong and at the same time so fleeting
up to the point that,
I do not know if you are real or not.

You probably only exist in my imagination
If it is imagination, Why such a strong feeling?

So, you are real but unreachable
So far from me...so silent, so indifferent...

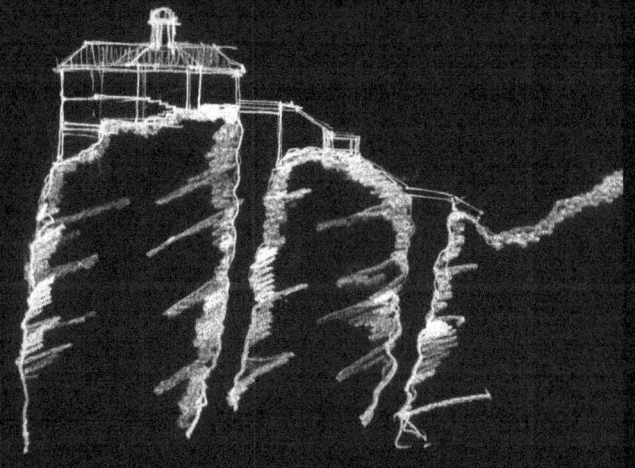

Ροσσάνου.

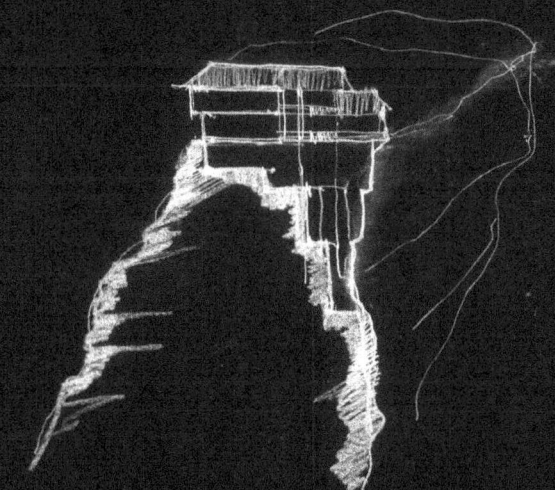

Monasteries Rossanou and Ag. Nikol Anapavsas Meteora

Αϊ Νικολάς Αναπαυσάς

II

...How I would like to meet you sometime.
At least four times each year
to hug you for an instant
once a season and kiss you for a second.

An affectionate and delicate kiss of eternity.

...in Autumn, I'd like to give you a kiss of color
that illuminates your heart

...in Summer, I'd like to give you a kiss of freshness
that refreshes your soul

...in Winter, I'd like to give you a kiss of warmth
that caress your spirit

...in Spring, I'd like to give you a kiss of fragrance
that perfumes your face

An affectionate and delicate kiss of eternity

How impossible it is to meet you...

How hard it is to get your attention...

How harsh is the way to reach you...

Monastery Ag. Nikolas Anapavsas - Meteora

III

...The stars in the heaven are many
How brilliant they are...!!!

One of them is you
the most beautiful, the most shinning
the most distant.

If I had a stair to elevate myself to the heaven,
I believe that I could meet you...
but you are so far, so unreachable,
so silent, so indifferent...oh my God

What impotence...!!!

If you could hear the sound of my voice,
the voice of my love...

My shout is probably so weak and insignificant
that you can't pay attention to it...

Why is a star, a point in the sky so strong,
so intense that it is able to transform your existence?

It is because of the power of its light,

It's the brightness of its presence.

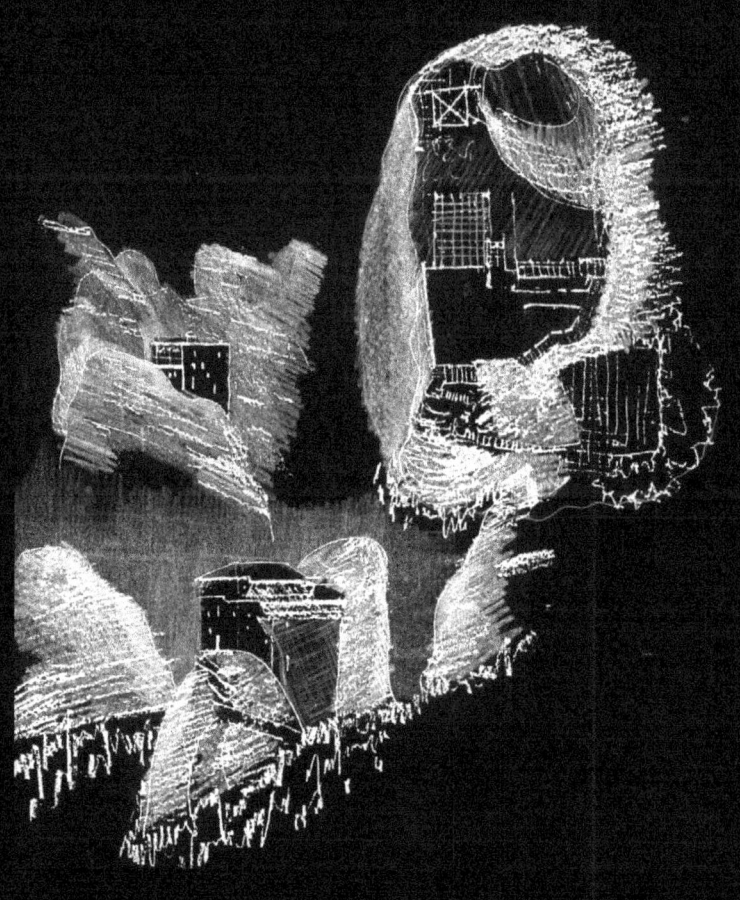

Monastery Ag. Nikolas Anapavsas - Meteora

IV

...I can see mount Olympus from my window
with all its gods and among the divinities is you,
so beautiful, so brilliant, so powerful and so unreachable

I don't exactly understand if your presence
is part of the mythology, or a torch of hope.

Oh my God...Is it probably an illusion?

If I could climb up the hillsides of your magnetic sweetness
and to reach the level of your wisdom
just to understand a little bit of your essence,
the essence which I love but...

I don't know how to express my love for you
to get your attention.

How uphill is the way to reach you,
and how tired and lost I feel..

Only if I had the strength to abandon you... but
it is so impossible...I love you so much.

If I could make my thoughts reality,
how happy I'd be.

Monastery Ag. Nikolas Anapaysas - Meteora

V

...Your physical presence is absence,
your spirit is omnipresence

Inspiration, imagination, creativity...
everything comes from you.

You are my inspiring ubiquity every time,
my spirit feels motivated by your existence.

Your absence is abstinence
and your presence happiness

You are in my heart...

Can you imagine how difficult it is
to take away from my mind
what is so rooted in my heart???

Oh no my God...I can't breathe...

What a strong and painful feeling...

I can't live without you...oh my love...!!!

Monastery Ag. Theodoron - Meteora

VI

...The waves of the sea carry
the sound of your sweet voice to me

The air of the beach caresses me
and I can feel your soft hand
inviting me for a dialogue

The smell of the breeze is
like the breath of your mouth close to me
ready for a kiss; a sweet, delicate kiss.

If I could be part of your essence,
how happy I'd be...I am prepared to respond,

I'm waiting, but...

This beautiful moment doesn't come.
Oh my God...how uphill is the way...

Where will I find patience...???
Where...???

Monastery Docheiariou - Mount Athos

VII

…How harsh is your silence,
your immutability how rigid it is.

I feel like a mendicant monk
praying to God for an inspiring word,

Your indifference is present,
your frosty reception is terrible
but your smile is life
your sweetness is balsam for my spirit

If you were able to hear me…

The closed wall of your heart,
opens the wound of my soul.

Your absence is like a desert without an oasis,
it is the strong experience of nothing,
it is absolute emptiness…

I wish you were here…
to feel the plenitude in my life

Monastery of Agia Monistav - Mount Athos

VIII

…My cosmos has changed in three days,
from the moment I meet you,
it is so difficult, practically impossible
to live without you

You are always on my mind, permanently,
at every moment, at every second.

I breathe your name,

I close my eyes just to see you clearer,
to contemplate your deepness.

If it could be possible to live without you,
it would be very nice,
but from the moment that you invaded my heart

I can't live without your presence,
your spiritual presence

Your physical presence is always absent,
your silent is implacable…

My anguish is so deep
my sadness is so big…
as deep and great as my love for you…

Monastery Ag. Dionysiou - Mount Athos

IX

...My words have been drawn in the sand,
they are blurring through time

but your image is so clear that I can touch it and kiss it.

My imagination,
without barriers can hug your presence

but like water in the hands
disappears very quickly
and my soul is again thirsty,
withered, almost dry...

Your inspiring presence doesn't want to disappear,

It is still here in my spirit

disillusion follows illusion...it doesn't matter,

it is worthwhile to hope...

it is important to wait...

it is necessary to pray...

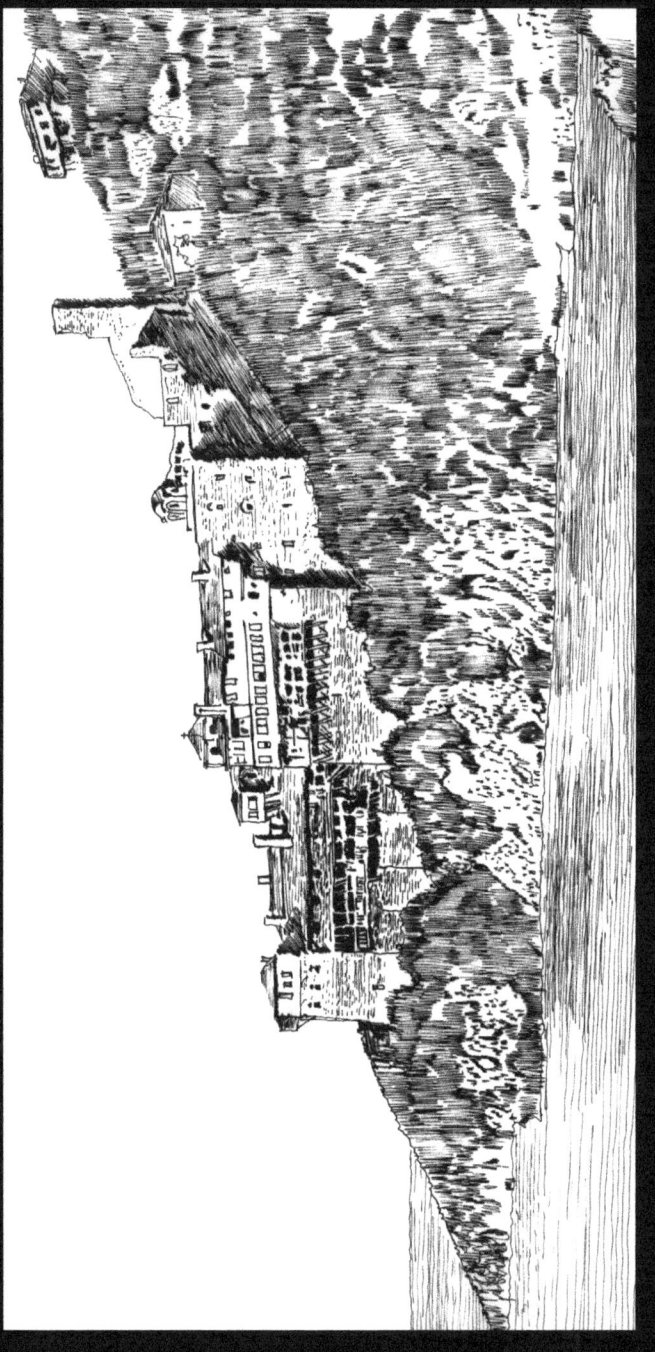

Monastery Grigoriou - Mount Athos

X

...How far is the way through the desert,
how dry is its atmosphere, like your absence,

My steps on the sand are so light
that you can't discern from the sky,

The sand, the sky, you the sun, my sun and I,
what a wilderness...what a silence... what loneliness...
just the sound of the wind
which carries the ultrasound of your voice to me,
so sweet, so soft, so deep, so volatile...

but your are far away from me, completely absent...

It is my imagination, my wish, my illusion, my expectation
there is no oasis in which I could meet you...
no horizon, just desert...emptiness...

In this experience of nothing
I have to learn to walk...without you...
although you are in my mind, my heart, my spirit...

You are my inspiration...

Monastery Nea Moni - Meteora

XI

...You don't give me a sign of life,
your silence is so lacerating ...
and your indifference so unbearable
that in your sweetness I detect bitterness

I'm so sad...I'm suffering so much...
the time without you is so intolerable...

If I could be liberated from these feelings
I'd probably be happier but not alive

I'm alive because of your existence...

Now, that I understand you
I realize that life is worthwhile...

You give me surprises, nice surprises, creative surprises...

If you disappear from my sight, I'll miss you too much...
My sweet Lady Arch when I meet you again...

I don't know what else I can do...
I feel confused even lost...

Monastery Nea Moni - Meteora

XII

...The sun goes down and I love you
I miss you, my inspiration fades away

the tiredness is interminable,
the sorrow is infinite,
my voice is extinguished...
my dreams are withered...

I'm so thirsty for you
my strengths are so weakened
and your existence is so powerful

your presence so volatile
and your absence so strong

the eternal desire to meet you,
finally it'll never come

and my hope slowly melts away,
gently evaporates...

tomorrow I'll probably feel stronger...

Monastery Nea Moni - Meteora

XIII

...From the sky a star has fallen
very close to me...
I didn't notice that it was you
What a distraction...!!!

When your presence disappeared
I could perceive how strong your light was
to enlighten my soul for entire days, weeks, months...
up to the point that I can't live without its light

How fruitful and magnetic your sweet being is,
sweet like the grapes in winter...

nevertheless my bitterness,
from dawn to dusk,
accompanies me...
and my expectations are
little by little being extinguished

Oh my God...!!!
I hope I do not die without seeing it again.

Monastery Philosofou - Gortinia

XIV

...The waves of the sea sing within you
and with them my soul comes and goes

The music of the pines pronounces your name
and in their movements, dance a waltz of happiness
your happiness

Show me the way to reach your being
all around me is confusion

your being gives me clarity, inspiration, happiness,
plenitude, fullness, life in abundance,
like the sun and the water to the earth.

The clouds travel far away up to your country
where I can't get to
I send you a message with them,
just to remind you that I'm alive,
I still exist
and I love you so much...

Monasteries Rossanou and Ag. Nikolas Anapavsas - Meteora

XV

...My heart throbs in silence
waiting for an answer,
like flowers expect spring.

The birds sing in the trees
calling their love
like I call upon your name.

Your blue scarf,
so soft, like your white skin,
hugs your neck as I'd like to do
but you are so distant, so far from me,
...almost unreachable

How I'd like to be a kite
to elevate my heart to your soul

Not even my words can reach your ears
let alone, reach your heart...

What despair...!!!

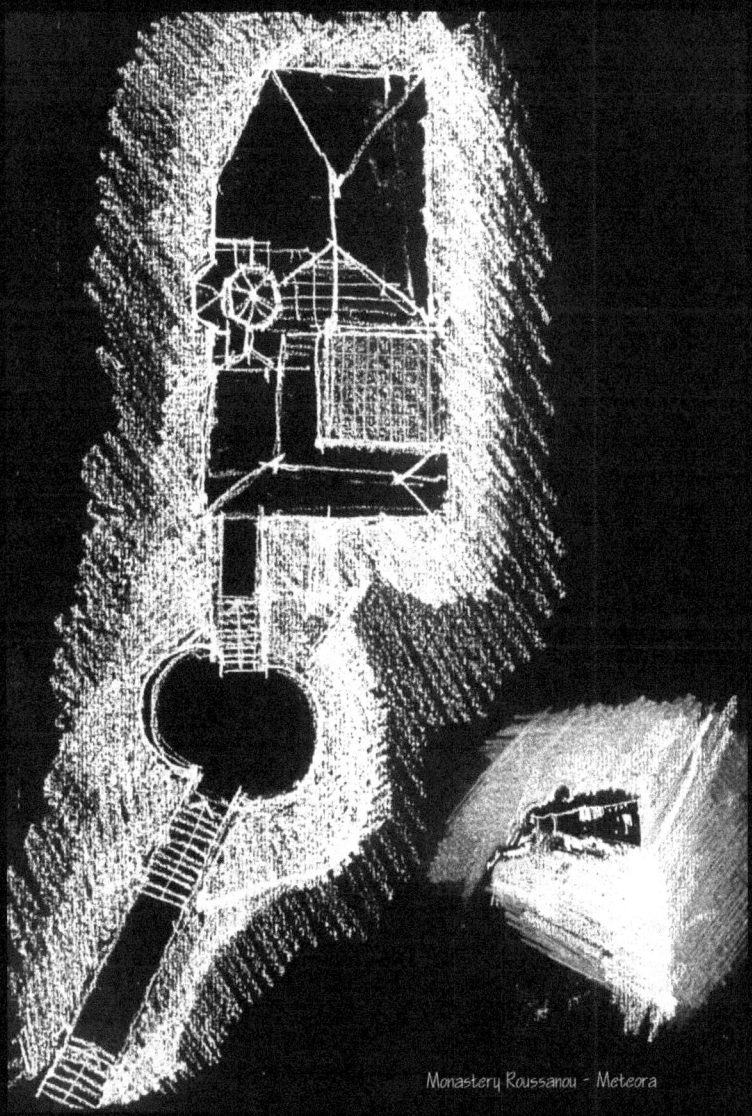

Monastery Roussanou - Meteora

XVI

...The words I pronounce in honor of your love
are not even mine,
they are yours if you want to hear them,
to meditate on them, to keep in your heart.

I'd like if you heard them as I wish,
as a sweet breeze whispering in your ear
with the fragrance
of the most beautiful flowers you love.

Now, I feel like the flowers of an almond tree
so sad during the winter of your indifference,
so happy under the sun of your smile.

These words I dedicate to you
climb up as ivy on the wall of my anguish.

The wind of this feeling
wrap up my soul as a whirlwind.

Monastery Roussanou - Meteora

XVII

...The immensity of the sky, mount Olympus,
the Aegean sea, a ship in front of me
and you inside me
in my heart, in my soul,
in my mind...

permanently flying through all my being
transforming my existence.

My sweet and colorful butterfly that
remembers me the coming of spring,
your presence is so fragile
that disappears when I try to hug you
when I try to kiss you.

All my words are colored
because of my love for you,
everything in my life,
is full of your presence.

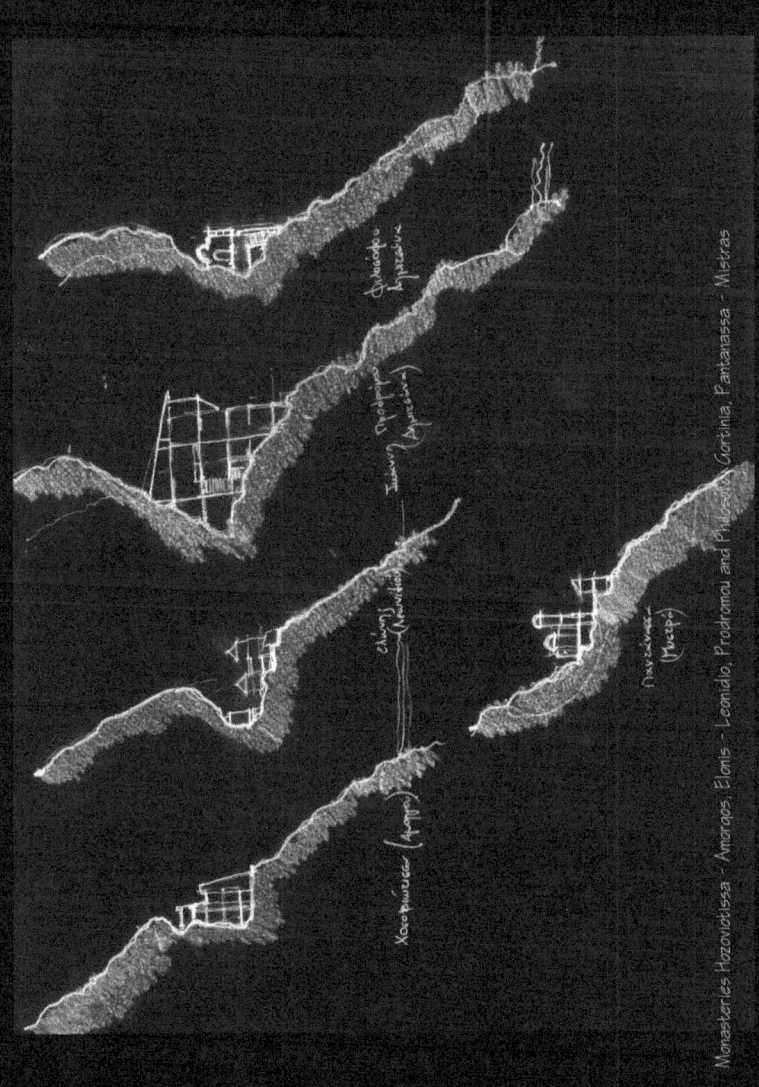

Monasteries Hozoviotissa - Amorgos, Elonis - Leonidio, Prodromou and Philosofou, Cortinia, Parkanassa - Mistras

XVIII

...The snow of the mountain
is melting when the spring comes
as I do when I think that
you are so distant from me

Nevertheless, it is also during spring
that flowers bloom,
as my desire to meet you again
just to whisper in your ear.

How essential you are for me
how much I love you

The birds sing your name
the waves of the sea sound the chorus
and the wind carries
the blurred image of your figure to me
so sweet, so delicate, so eternal...

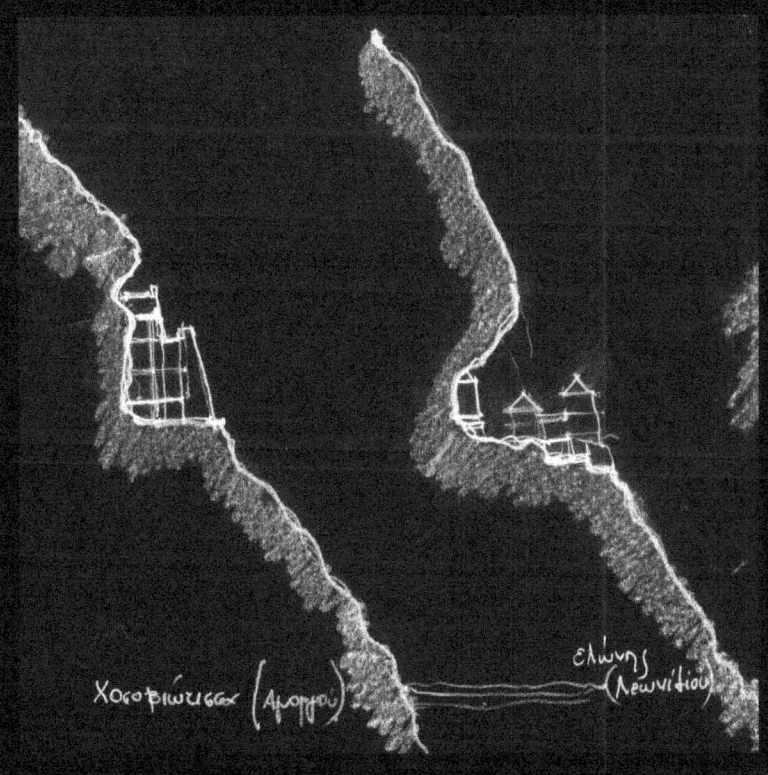

Monasteries Hozoviotissa - Amorgos and Elonis - Leonidio

XIX

...I remember you,
as you were in winter,
dressed in black on your white skin
the soft blue scarf around your neck
and your permanent sweet smile.

I have seen my eyes in your eyes,
both of us walking on the snow
with quick steps, talking, observing,
becoming familiar each other,

what a beautiful surprise...
I remember clearly,
it was Wednesday in January.

My heart flies again back through time
to meet you in the future.

What a sweet remembrance
like the honey that springs up from your eyes
like the words that come out of your lips.

You are a fresh rose in my desert life.

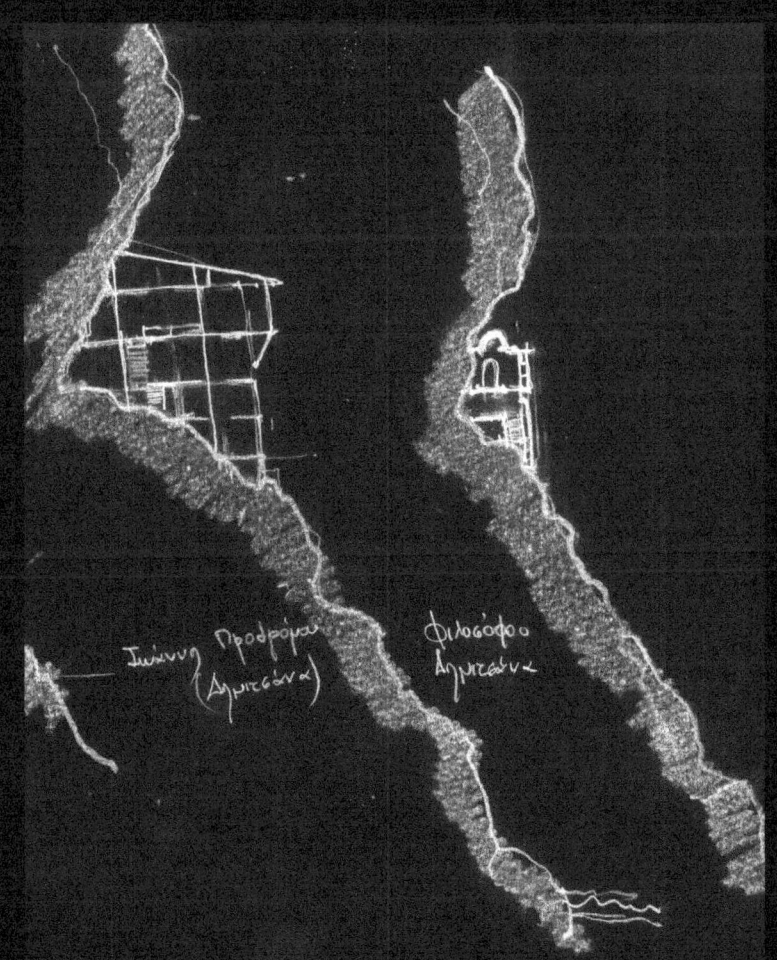

Monasteries Prodromou and Philosofou - Gortinia

XX

...High, very high
in the dark blue sky of winter
a white moon is shinning intensely,

I can contemplate with it
the brightness of your eyes,
the pureness of your smile
the whiteness of your face
on the gloomy back of my loneliness.

I don't understand,
all my love appears suddenly,
now that you are far from me,

I'm so sad and you so oblivious.
How I'd like to know that
you are aware of my pure love for you

I know this love is unrequited
just esteem it, respect it.
Don't be indifferent...

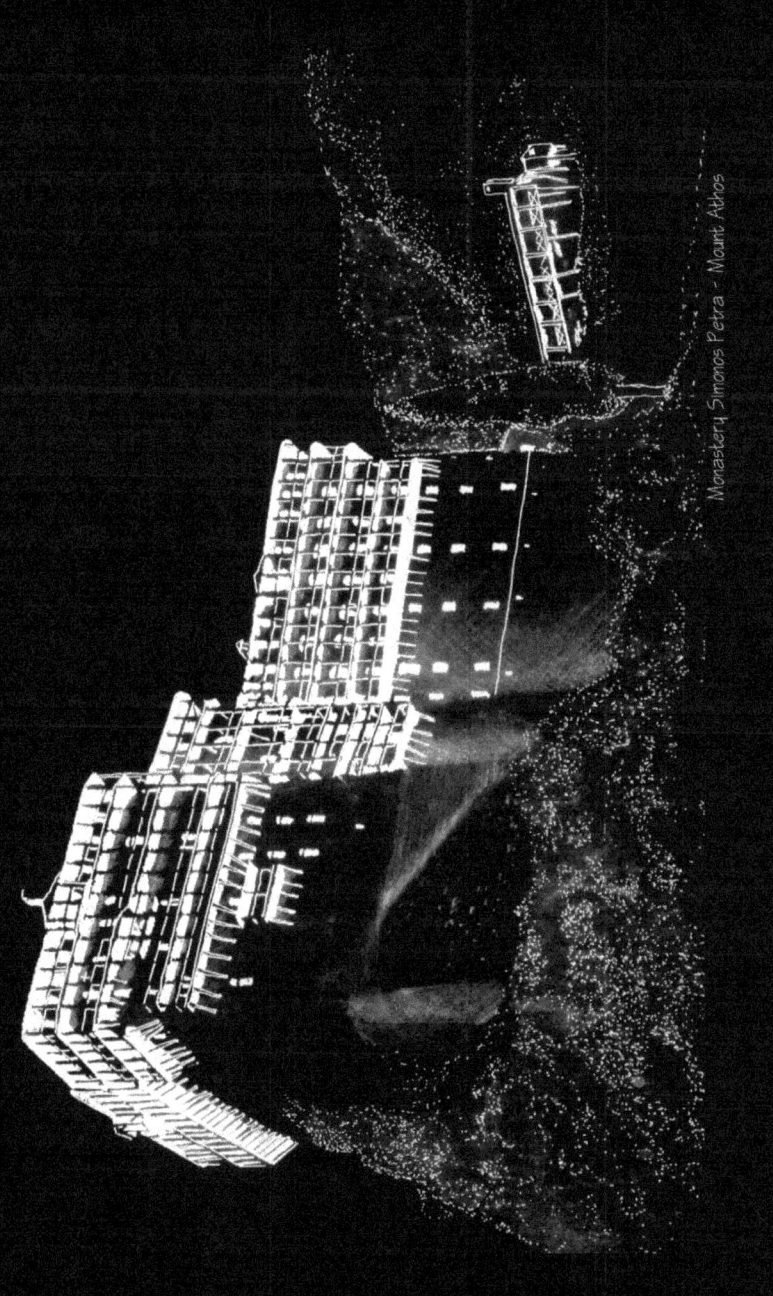

Monastery Simonos Petra - Mount Athos

XXI

...Dusk is coming, a sad sun is disappearing
behind Olympus.

You are going to enlighten another heart
I'll be waiting for you to come,

the dawn of the next day is not so far...
the stars will be my solace
they will accompany me
together with the music of the pines.

During the dark and silent night of your absence
the dew bathe my illusion,

it's like a balsam for my anguished heart.

My shinning sun of the north...
don't be late, don't be late...

I'm still here...waiting for you.

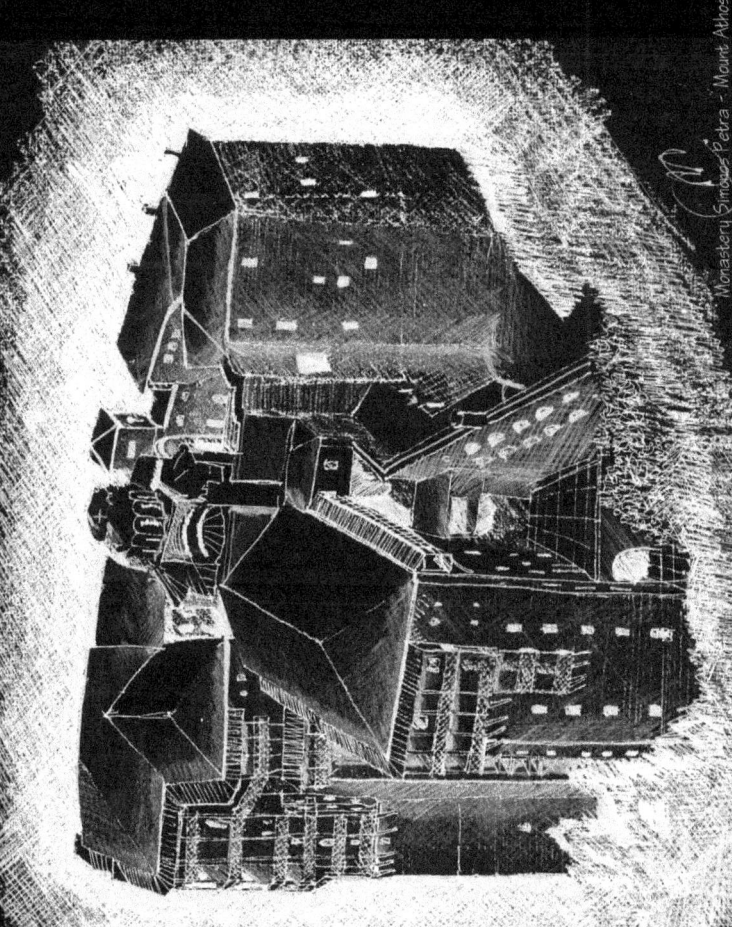

Monastery Simonos Petra - Mount Athos

XXII

...What a dusty treasure existed in my soul
when you reached to me

I was probably waiting for you
without knowing it,

Hence the surprise,
but what a nice surprise...

I'd like to know that
what was asleep in your soul
could be awaken up by my words,
my gestures, my love.

You are my daily energy that comes
like the dew to roses in spring,

you are the refuge of my soul,
the light of my days

my inspiring source...

Monastery Simonos Petra - Mount Athos

XXIII

...You are tall and lively
like the silvered pines of the south.

You are incomparable,
so sweet, so special, so unique.

I write your name on the sand,
but nobody knows how much I love you

it's invisible and simultaneously so sorrowful.

The furious wind of my anguish
tries to kill my love for you,

but this one on the contrary

like coal extinguishing
suddenly catches fire in rebellion
refusing to die, like the morning star...

which with the dawn
wants to kiss your existence...

Monastery Simonos Petra - Mount Athos

XXIV

...I'd like to do with you
what the spring does with the flowers,
she gives life just with a breath.

You don't hear my voice,

you don't feel my breath
and you continue being a flower
you don't need me...

but I need the sun of your spring
not to wither
like the vine arbor in autumn.

Colorful butterfly of my dreams
don't stop fluttering in my soul.

Your sweet presence emerges in my spirit
like the water in the desert,
so fresh, so natural, so vital...

Monastery Simonos Petra - Mount Athos

XXV

...Life is so short,
just a holiday between
eternity and eternity.

Eternity of hope before we are born,
eternity of reflection after we've died.

It is so poor to live this short time without love,
which is part of eternity.

The hate, the rancor, the indifference
must not have a place in this game, so
why does it exist in you?

Don't cultivate these kind of feelings
It is not worthwhile,
I'm so small, so insignificant
I just want to be an architect.

Life, please give me the opportunity to be...
You have gave me the chance to live...

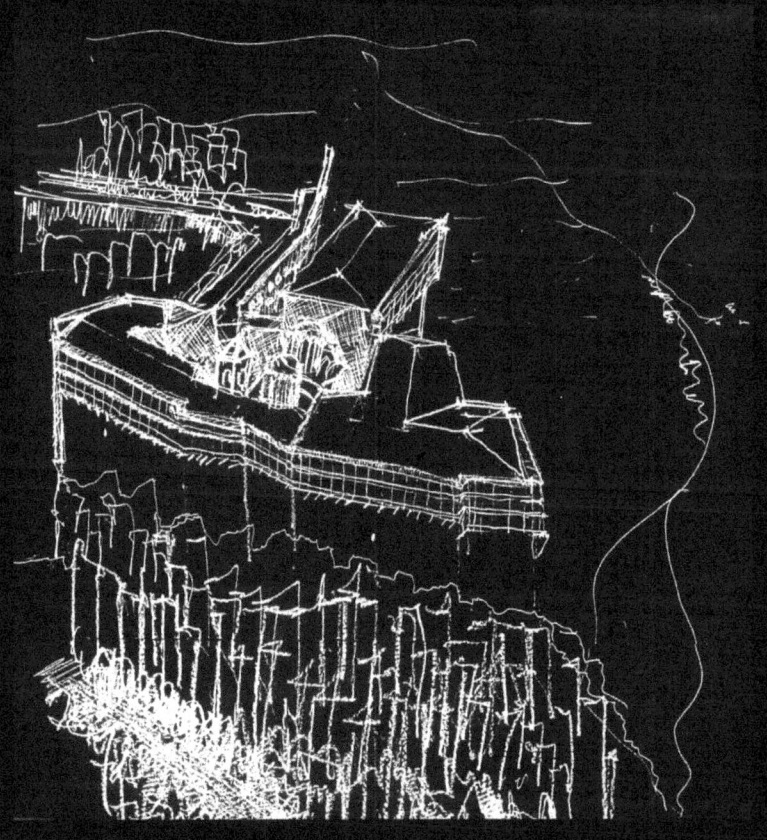

Monastery Simonos Petra - Mount Athos

XXVI

...Some drops emerge from the rocks
Are they crying?

Like the tears have been trying
to escape from my eyes
Are they crying?

Rocks don't cry
but my heart does, it isn't a stone.

A flower sprouts from the crevice of a rock
It is a shout of hope,
like my love is for you
which springs up from my heart.

I'd like to hear from a star in heaven
a message of your voice saying
that you love me as I love you.

But you, like the stars in heaven
are so silent, so distant, so indifferent...!!!

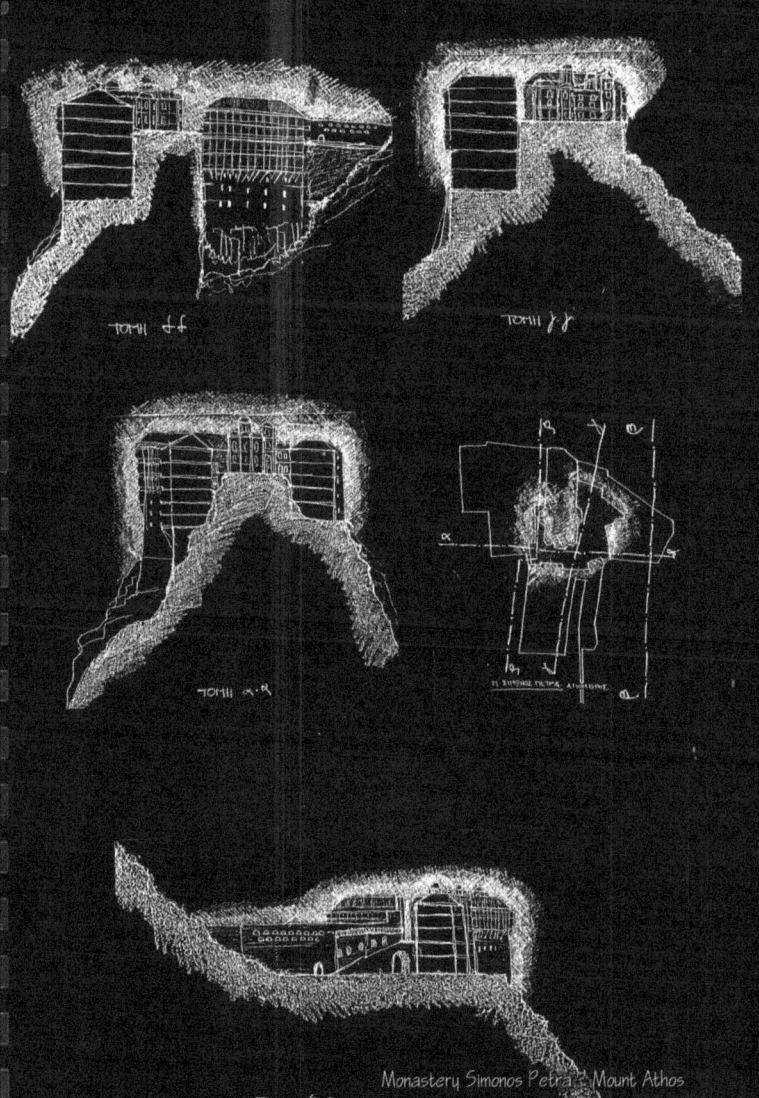

Monastery Simonos Petra - Mount Athos

XXVII

... My eternal dreams are alive
in your existence.

In your physical existence
the earthly dreams.

In your spiritual essence
the infinite dreams,
that's why the love is eternal,
it never dies

I elevate my gaze to the immense heaven
to meet you among the stars

I know you are there, hidden but present,

I feel your presence in my heart,
so strongly that it is impossible for me to breathe

you have taken my breath away...

but how strange, at the same time
you have revived me...

Monastery Ag. Ioanni Prodromou - Serres

XXVIII

...You are a song of dusk
that blossoms in my loneliness,

which accompanies me
when night falls
and the darkness of the sky
embraces me.

I wish you were a bird
and not a kite
although both fly through the sky;

The kite needs the string to come back
the bird, just the heart.

Olympus tries to hide you,
but in vain,
the horizon intends to create a barrier,
but fruitless
the sea attempts to refrain my impetus
without success...

this love has no frontiers...

Monastery Ag. Ioann Prodromou - Serres

XXIX

...The dust of times
will cover everything through eternity.

The ashes of our bodies
will be hovering in the air for years
like the leaves of the trees in autumn

but my love for you will be alive evermore
and floating forever in the wind of eternity.

Our souls will understand that
although you probably don't want to accept it.

And my soul will always be
looking forward to an answer
until the end of times.

and then,
I will not have your hands
but I will relish your smile...

Monastery Ag. Ioanni Prodromou - Serres

XXX

...If my love for you could join
my being with your existence,

like the line of the horizon does
with the sky and the earth

How content I'd be.

But all I have from you
is your silence, your indifference.

I hope you never suffer for anyone,
the way I'm suffering for you,
the pain is lacerating.

All of my words intend to fill
the emptiness that your absence
leaves in me.

In the rainbow I can see your sweet face
framing my blue sky that is you...

Monastery Ag. Ioanni Prodromou - Serres

XXXI

...I'd like to give you just one kiss
the most delicate, tender,
the longest, sweetest,
this one, the unique,

which will accompany you
for all of eternity.

You are the light that lead me
because you are a star.

This star makes me weep
but these tears are the most beautiful.

Oh! my sweet and colorful butterfly,
I wait in silence and with patience
the moment you will alight on my shoulder,

that day will be the happiest of my life
I'll flavor the joyfulness on my lips
I'll feel the happiness in my spirit...

XXXII

...Distant and Inexpressive
as if your were dead.

Please smile at me, talk to me
I'll see that you are alive...

So, my soul will be back in my being,
and the happiness will inundate my heart.

Oh! creator of my solitary dreams
when will I meet you again?

I expect of this wonderful moment,
in the dusk of spring day

waiting together for the moon, in the sea,
with our hands joined until dawn...
don't make me wait for too long.

I need your breath,
to be able to breathe...

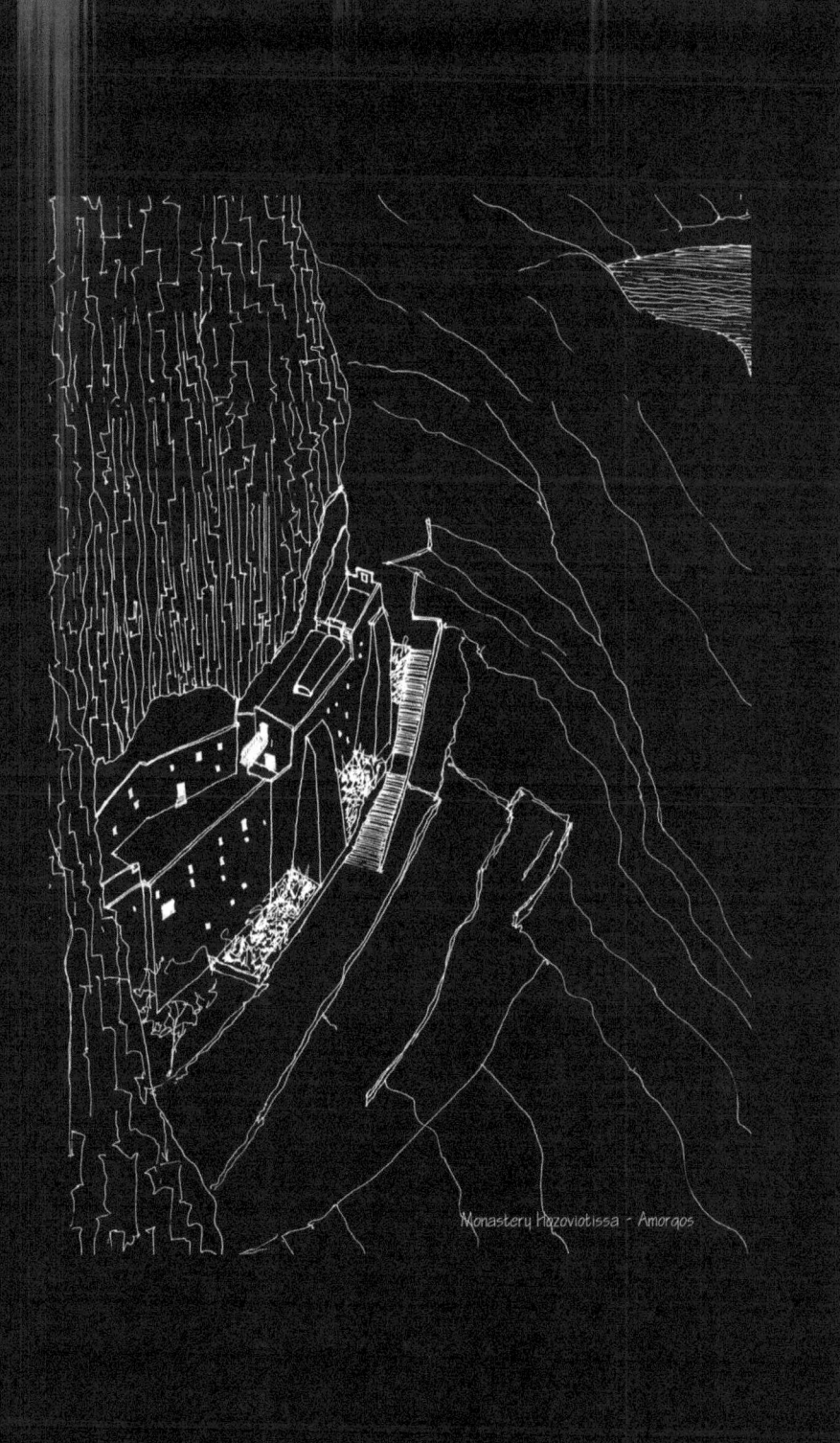

XXXIII

...You are like a solitary cloud
in the blue sky

I like your color, your form,
your resilience, your way, your freedom.

You cannot hide the sun,
because you are also the sun, my sun.

The breeze of dusk makes you disappear.
I hope to meet you again at dawn.

I feel revived under the sun
from your sweet smile and your tender gaze.

I'd like to mill my hopes
my distant hopes, my shady hopes

but I can't...
it's impossible to erase you from my mind,
even more difficult
to make you disappear from my heart...

Monastery Hozoviotisa - Amorgos

XXXIV

...You are like the delirious butterfly's fluttering,
and the imperious strength of sea waves.

The natural slenderness of your figure is
like the lilies of the valley

so fresh, so lively, so beautiful.

My soul is thirsty for you.

How terrible it is to bear
the heavy night without you.

These phrases come so naturally
on the paper
like the nocturnal dew on the prairie.

Your happiness is my happiness.
Your sadness is my sadness.

I'd like to contribute to make you greater,
more innovated, more important,
more transcendental...

Monastery Hozoviotissa - Amorgos

XXXV

...My heart is looking for her
but in vain, she isn't here.
The wind carried her away.

These will be the last verses I'm writing

My strengths have become weaker,
It doesn't matter, as long as I can breathe
I will be waiting for her.

I hope before dying
to leave my heart in her hands.

The heart with which I loved
from the moment I meet her.

Many people have loved her,
have dedicated much time to her
very fruitful, more than me...

But the deepness of my love, so platonic
so pure, so transparent...
I don't know if it is comparable to something similar.
This was my destiny, my eagerness, my yearning

But everything has fallen into a deep well.
Everything has been disintegrated in the air.

Everything has become a wreck.

Nothing is present, just emptiness...
Any way, it was worth the attempt

It's time to leave, good bye.
God bless her, God forgive me.
Life must go on...!!!

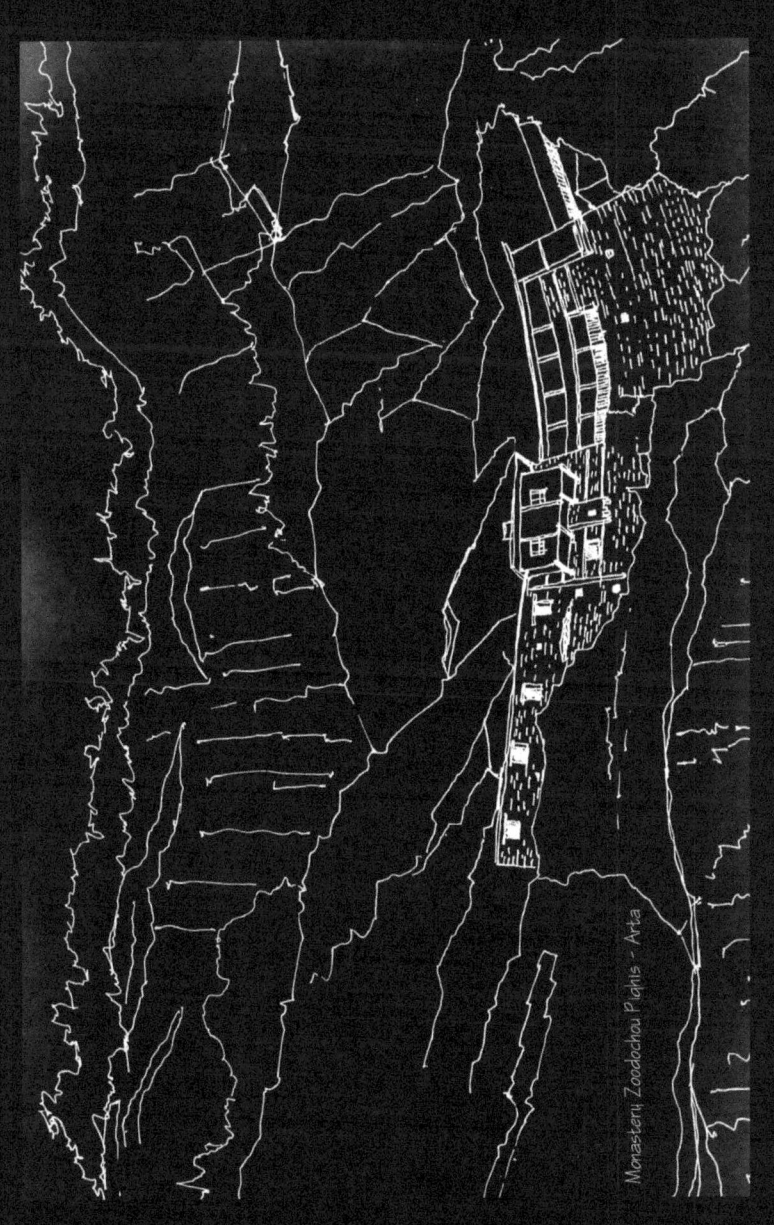

Monasteri Zoodochou Pighis - Arta

www.ingramcontent.com/pod-product-compliance
Lightning Source LLC
Chambersburg PA
CBHW061658040426
42446CB00010B/1795